HOW CHRISTIANS MADE PEACE WITH WAR

PEACE·AND·JUSTICE·SERIES 2

HOW CHRISTIANS MADE PEACE WITH WAR

Early Christian Understandings of War

JOHN DRIVER

HERALD PRESS
Scottdale, Pennsylvania
Kitchener, Ontario

Driver, John, 1924-
  How Christians made peace with war : early Christian
understandings of war / John Driver.
      p.   cm. — (Peace and justice series : 2)
  Bibliography: p.
  ISBN 0-8361-3461-3 (pbk.)
    1. War—Religious aspects—Christianity—History of doctrines-
-Early church, ca. 30-600.   2. Peace—Religious aspects-
-Christianity—History of doctrines—Early church, ca. 30-600.
  I. Title.   II.   Series.
BT736.2D74 1988   87-32908
241'.6242'09015—dc19

Unless otherwise indicated, Scripture references are from the *Good
News Bible*. Old Testament copyright © American Bible Society 1976;
New Testament copyright © American Bible Society 1966, 1971, 1976.

HOW CHRISTIANS MADE PEACE WITH WAR

Library of Congress Catalog Card Number: 87-32908
International Standard Book Number: 0-8361-3461-3
Printed in the United States of America
Design by Gwen Stamm/Paula M. Johnson

88 89 90 91 92 93 94 95 96 10 9 8 7 6 5 4 3 2 1

To
brothers and sisters
in the two-thirds world
who are seeking peace and justice
under conditions similar
to those experienced
by the early
Christians

Contents

Foreword

How can we achieve peace in our personal lives, our families, our communities, our world? Perhaps no topic leans more heavily on us today than this one, for it touches every area of our lives.

Our answer to it is influenced by a variety of factors. One of the major ones informing our response comes from leaders of the past, especially persons of political and religious stature.

While political and religious leaders today often look to military solutions to conflict, these increase tension rather than reduce it. Violence too often begets only more violence. In this book, author John Driver looks to history for another way—a peaceful resolution of conflict. He shows us how in the period from about A.D. 90 until 313, early Christians opposed warfare because of the life and teachings of Jesus. Jesus taught love for enemies, with a goal of bringing them to faith and friendship in God's family, the church. This led early Christians to extend love and forgiveness to persecutors and to call evildoers to a new way of life. However, through the years, Christians slowly became involved in military life until they lost their peaceful approach to solving conflict. John Driver, biblical scholar, prolific writer, and mission leader, shows us briefly and concisely how this change occurred.

How Christians Made Peace with War is the second book in a series on peace and justice themes. It provides a basis for thinking new thoughts about achieving peace in our times. Other titles in the series are listed at the back of the book. For more about early Christian attitudes and responses to war, check the references in the back of the book.

—J. Allen Brubaker, editor
Peace and Justice Series

How Christians
Made Peace with War

Introduction

Our survey of early Christian understandings of war covers the period between the close of the New Testament era (shortly before A.D. 100) and 313. It reaches beyond the year of the Emperor Constantine's edict of toleration in 313. His order marked a new era for the Christian church's attitude toward military service. From then on, Christians began to serve actively in the military in obedience to the state. This book will explore how Christian thinkers and church leaders of the period interpreted the meaning of this Constantinian shift.

You may ask why we should study the attitude of the early church toward war and militarism. Evangelical Christians resist interpreting the life and teaching of the church with previously established standards. This should not blind us, however, to the value of the practice and teaching of the early church regarding questions of militarism and warfare. Our world is quite distant from the social situation, customs, and thought patterns of the first century. This increases our difficulty in understanding the writings of the New Testament. Christians of that era were closer in time to the New Testament. The early believers read the New Testament writings in the same language in which they were written. They also lived in a world similar to the one in which the Christian church arose.

Although they were not always faithful to their Christian calling, it is helpful to see how they interpreted the New Testament. Of course, we should certainly not equate the writings of the early church leaders with the gospel. They surely contain, though, as much gospel truth as the writings of Christians of our own time whom we highly respect.

It is noteworthy that between 100 and 313 no Christian writers, to our knowledge, approved of Christian participation in warfare. In fact, all those who wrote on the subject disapproved of the practice.

However, the position of the church in this regard was not absolute. For example, some Christians who served in the Roman army were not for that reason excluded from the church's fellowship. From the close of the New Testament period until about A.D. 170, however, no firm evidence has surfaced that shows Christians serving in the army. From about 173 onward we find a gradually increasing number of Christians in the Roman army. At first, no doubt, they were mainly soldiers who had become Christians and simply remained in the army. Later, this group increasingly included Christians who had become soldiers.

The actual behavior of Christians during this period sometimes contradicted the church's vision. This difference is reflected in the writings of early church leaders. Sadly enough, this has often been the case. Throughout the history of the church, we observe the tension between the teaching of the church and the practice of Christians. These compromises are more often than not signs of human weakness and sin in the church.

The early church did resist the temptation to lower its teaching to the level of its practice. The convictions of early Christians were without doubt nonviolent. They had to struggle, however, to remain faithful to the Lord in the midst of a changing social situation.

The objections of early Christians to warfare and military service were based in the teachings and example of Jesus. This led them to resist stubbornly the evils and the injustices of their time. But in doing this, they resolutely refused to respond to evildoers with violence. They were even willing to suffer persecution and death rather than to shed the blood of their persecutors. Respecting the lives of their enemies, they refused to contribute to the vicious spiral of violence.

These early Christians also refused military service because they rejected idolatry. While they recognized the need of human government for justice and peace, they saw a fundamental opposition between Caesar and God. Therefore, they steadfastly refused to take part in the pagan ceremonies connected with Roman army life. On a deeper level, they rejected the claims of the emperor and his army for their unquestioning loyalty and obedience.

CHAPTER 1

The New Testament Roots of Nonviolence

According to the New Testament, Jesus gave considerable direct attention to nonviolence. However, since the earliest times, Christians have not agreed in their attitudes toward war and peace. We find hints of this difference already in the New Testament. In the history of the church since then, such differences have increased.

The attitude of Jesus is reflected in his command to love the enemy and not resist evil persons (Matthew 5:38-48; Luke 6:27-36). Paul's counsel to the Christians at Rome was:

> Bless those who persecute you; bless and do not curse them. . . . Repay no one evil for evil . . . so far as it depends upon you, live peaceably with all. Beloved, never avenge yourselves, but leave it to the wrath of God. . . . Do not be overcome by evil, but overcome evil with good. Romans 12:14,17-21 (RSV)

This advice, written about A.D. 60, was surely derived from Jesus' teaching. Paul's version of Jesus' attitude agrees, on the whole, with the Lord's teaching recorded by Matthew and Luke some 20 years later. These texts show that Jesus did not limit his call to love and nonviolence to the inner attitudes of the disciple. He deals rather with the effect of nonviolence on the enemy. So the love Jesus here commanded has concrete social importance.

Some New Testament texts may seem to point in another direction. For example, we notice that the actions of the disciples disagree with Jesus' teachings on nonviolence. They advocated calling down divine vengeance on their enemies. On the very eve of Jesus' crucifixion there were swords in their midst. (See Luke 9:54; Mark 14:47.) Military persons sometimes appear in the Gospels without any specific questioning of their military service.

Though Jesus used many metaphors and parables, he drew none of them from military life. A possible exception to this statement occurs in Luke 14:31-33. However, it is not the troops here who furnish examples for the followers of Jesus, but the decision of the king based on political and military considerations. Paul uses many military expressions in his writings.

In the writings of the early church, we notice an increased use of military metaphors for all aspects of the life of the church. Even those church leaders who spoke forcefully against Christian participation in warfare freely used military metaphors for the church. Cyprian, bishop of the church in Carthage from the year 250, compared the church to an army camp. Here the soldiers of Christ are trained and sent into battle against the adversary.[1]

The early Christians clearly held Jesus' teachings on love

and nonviolence. This may account for their ability to make ample use of military metaphors without undercutting their opposition to war. However, changing social and political conditions gradually led the church to take these teachings with less seriousness. In this situation, the use of military metaphors actually served to support the participation of Christians in warfare. First, soldiers of Christ also became soldiers of the emperor. Later, in the Middle Ages, Christians formed an actual army, known as the Crusaders.

The New Testament commands to "love your enemies" and to "bless those who persecute you" express an active missionary concern for enemies and persecutors. In Romans 12:14-21, the response of active love toward violent persons is aimed at reconciling them. Evil persons can only be overcome with good. To love and to practice nonviolence toward enemies is not a question of good judgment. Rather, it follows the way God has chosen to communicate his saving good news (Matthew 5:45). To love the enemy through genuine expressions of nonviolence and self-giving generosity is to be merciful as God is merciful (Luke 6:35-37).

In the early centuries of the church, Christians who suffered wrong without resistance at the hands of their enemies and persecutors were called "confessors" and "martyrs." *Martyr* in Greek means "witness." Martyrs were persons who had given the ultimate witness. They were willing to suffer death rather than use violence to defend or avenge themselves. Martyrdom, therefore, meant much more than simply resisting pressures to deny the faith. When these Christians refused to resort to the violence of revolution or self-defense, they were being faithful to their missionary call. They sought to make disciples of all nations. They also sought to communicate salvation to their persecutors as God in Christ shows love to his enemies. Suffering and martyrdom in the early church were neither meaningless nor absurd. They grew out of a confrontation between two systems of contrasting values and conflicting loyalties. Persistent resistance to evil, linked with a nonresistant love for evildoers, produced many martyrs in the early church.

The missionary aspect of nonviolence is shown in the resistance of confessors to evil. Many suffered imprisonment and torture, exile and loss of goods, persecutions against family members, and all sorts of harassment. During periods of intense persecution, confessors condemned to forced labor in the mines of Cerdeña were cared for economically by their brothers and sisters in the church in Rome. To suffer and die for their faith by no means meant indifference to suffering or a stoic sense of resignation. It was the ultimate proof of courage and valor. In fact, writers of the period used images drawn from combat in the arena to describe their suffering and martyrdom.

Probably not all the early Christians who suffered persecution and martyrdom were conscious of how their nonresistant suffering communicated the gospel. And some, we may imagine, were anything but nonviolent in their attitude toward their persecutors. Even so, nonresistant suffering and martyrdom communicated the faith effectively. The saying attributed to Tertullian—"the blood of the martyrs has become the seed of the church"— reflects the situation accurately. Many testimonies point to the effective witness of the martyrs. Occasionally, the persecutors themselves joined the martyrs in their witness unto death.

As Origen later argued, the church can perform its priesthood for society only through nonviolence. This specific service to the world requires a holiness which separates the people of God from the rest of society. Therefore, Christians dare not shed blood through violence as the world does.[2]

The prophets spoke of a mountaintop city to which Gentile nations would come. This biblical image is important for understanding the mission of God's people. Isaiah 2:1-4 and Micah 4:1-4 speak of the mountain of the house of the Lord rising above all other mountains. In the age of the Messiah, the people of God will shine forth as God's model society. And to this city the nations of all the earth will stream to experience God's saving social order. In these prophetic texts, the most important characteristic of this new order is nonviolence.

> They will hammer their swords into plows and their spears into pruning knives. Nations will never again go to war, never prepare for battle again. (Isaiah 2:4)

Jesus applied this missionary vision of God's people to the disciples gathered around him (Matthew 5:14-16). All the early church leaders who wrote on this subject agreed that the prophetic vision was being fulfilled in their midst. Through Christ and the Christian community, the word of the Lord had gone forth. God's new social order had been manifested. The house of the Lord was visible above all other hills. Now the nations of the world could come streaming into the house of God. The Gentile church was emerging from the witness shining forth from the messianic community.

The witness of this Christian community was very attractive. Why? Because the nonviolence and peace envisioned by the prophets had already become a reality in the church. Between the years 150 and 250, the principal church leaders all shared this vision: Justin Martyr,[3] Irenaeus,[4] Tertullian,[5] and Origen.[6] Tertullian, for example, interpreted the prophetic vision of messianic peace with these words, "Who else, therefore, are understood but we who, fully taught by the new law, observe these practices."[7] And Origen commented, "For we no longer take up 'sword against nation,' nor do we 'learn war anymore,' having become children of peace for the sake of Jesus."[8]

The Jews charged that if nothing had changed in the world, the Messiah could not have come according to Isaiah 2:4. And since the world is still filled with war, Jesus of Nazareth cannot have been the Messiah. These church leaders responded to the charges of their critics, admitting that the world indeed brims with violence. They also agreed with the Jews that the coming of the Messiah would indeed change the world.

On the other hand, they rejected the idea that redemption would come at the end of the world. They also refused to believe that because salvation takes place invisibly, the world need not be changed. Christians adopted such ideas about 200 years later when nonviolence was no longer the expected character of the church.

The early church leaders, therefore, answered that the Messiah had already come and that the world had in fact changed. It had been transformed in the people of the Messiah who live according to the law of Christ. There was no longer any violence in the messianic people, the church.

They had become "children of peace." In the church, the making of war was being unlearned.

The prophetic vision was being fulfilled in the church. According to these early church leaders, nonviolence was an authentic part of the missionary witness of the church. Because these early Christians rejected war, their concern to bring others into the Christian community was believable.

CHAPTER 2

The Earliest Church Leaders

Christian writers in the period following the New Testament era agreed in their praise of peace and their opposition to warfare. Ignatius of Antioch wrote in about 110, "Nothing is more precious than peace, by which all war, both in heaven and earth, is brought to an end."[9] In the context of the violence in which early Christians lived, he offered this counsel: "Do not avenge yourselves on those who injure you ... let us imitate the Lord, who when he was reviled, reviled not again; when he was crucified, he answered not; when he suffered, he threatened not, but prayed for his enemies."[10]

Clement of Rome wrote around the year 95. In one prayer, he asked that justice and peace might reign and that all people might submit themselves to God and to the Messiah. Then he added, "Give concord and peace to us and to all who inhabit the earth as Thou gavest to our fathers ... we being obedient to Thy almighty and most excellent Name and to our rulers and governors upon the earth."[11]

Polycarp, in a brief summary of the Christian life, wrote,

"Not rendering evil for evil, or railing for railing, or blow for blow, or cursing for cursing."[12]

Athenagoras, writing in about 180, expressed the same vision in his *Plea for Christians*[13] He also affirmed the sacredness of human life. "We [Christians] cannot endure even to see a man put to death, though justly."[14] (He was referring to the circus games which he forbade Christians to attend.)

Abortion and infanticide, both common practices in that period, were also completely out of the question for Christians. This attitude naturally implied refusal to kill in warfare, since Christians consistently respected human life.[15] At about the same time, Clement of Alexandria wrote, "We Christians are a peaceful race . . . for it is not in war, but in peace, that we are trained."[16]Justin Martyr, a Greek who spoke in defense of nonviolence, wrote the following in about 153. "We who formerly used to murder one another do not only now refrain from making war upon our enemies, but also that we may not lie nor deceive our examiners, die willingly confessing Christ."[17] He also wrote that Christians who once

> were filled with war, and mutual slaughter, and every wickedness, have each through the whole earth changed our warlike weapons—our swords into plowshares and our spears into implements of tillage—and we cultivate piety, righteousness, philanthropy, faith and hope, which we have from the Father himself through him who was crucified.[18]

Justin viewed Christians as without doubt a people of peace. He saw that the prophetic vision of Micah 4:1-4 had begun to be fulfilled in the Christians. In reality, Justin was the first of a whole series of early Christian writers who shared this view.

Later, in the second century, Theophilus became bishop of Antioch. He was the first writer who had the official authority of the church to express a similar conviction.[19] Irenaeus became bishop of Lyons toward the end of the second century. He also said that the vision of Micah 4 and Isaiah 2 was already being fulfilled.

> But if the law of liberty—that is, the Word of God— preached by the apostles [who went forth from Jerusalem] throughout all the earth caused such a change in the state of things, that these [nations] did form their swords and warlances into plowshares and ... pruning hooks ... [that is] into instruments used for peaceful purposes, and that they are now unaccustomed to fighting, but when smitten, offer the other cheek, then the prophets have not spoken these things of any other person, but of Him who effected them. This person is our Lord.[20]

At about the same time, Tertullian, the North African theologian, wrote:

> And they shall join to beat their [swords] into plows, and their lances into sickles; and nations shall not take up [sword] against nation, and they shall no more learn to fight. Who else, therefore, are understood but we who fully taught by the new law observe these practices—the old law being obliterated, the coming of whose abolition the action itself [of beating swords into plows, etc.] demonstrates? For the custom of the old law was to avenge itself by the vengeance of the sword, and to pluck out "eye for eye" and to inflict retaliatory revenge for injury. But the new law's custom is to point to clemency, and to convert to tranquility

the primitive ferocity of "swords" and "lances" and to remodel primitive execution of "war" upon the rivals and foes of the law into pacific actions of "plowing" and "tilling" the land.[21]

Cyprian, a bishop in North Africa and a disciple of Tertullian, clearly supported the same theme a few decades later. "And God willed iron to be used for the culture of the earth, but not on that account must murders be committed."[22]

At about the same time Origen, who lived in Egypt and Palestine, expressed his understanding of this vision in the following words:

> And to those who inquire of us whence we come, or who is our founder, we reply that we are come, agreeably to the counsels of Jesus, to "cut down our hostile and insolent 'wordy' swords into ploughshares, and to convert into pruning hooks the spears formerly employed in war." For we no longer take up "sword against nation." Nor do we "learn war any more," having become children of peace, for the sake of Jesus, who is our leader.[23]

These representative Christian authors all wrote between the years 150 and 250. They reflect the view which apparently characterized the church throughout the Roman Empire during this period. Their writings came from Rome and Palestine, from southern France and North Africa. They all reflect the sense of identity which marked the Christian church, the restored people of God.

In these people, the messianic vision of the prophets has already begun to be fulfilled. They were faithful to the example and teachings of Jesus. Their obedience to his Spirit present in the church made this vision a reality in their midst. The whole world would not recognize this sovereignty until the last day. But believers had no reason or excuse to disregard the new way of peace which marked this kingdom begun by Christ, the Messiah. Even after Constantine had gained power in the Roman Empire, Christians continued to write about the fulfillment of the prophetic vision.

However, there were fundamental differences. Eusebius of Caesarea, historian and advocate for the faith under Constantine, expressed his convictions in his writing.

> That which the prophecies foretold has been fulfilled precisely. The various independent governments were destroyed by the Romans; and Augustus became the sole master of the entire universe at the very moment when our Savior came down to earth. Since that time, no nation has waged war on another nation, and life is no longer squandered in the former confusion.[24]

> [Since the coming] of Jesus, there is no longer a multiplicity of sovereigns reigning over the world's peoples.[25]

According to Eusebius, the peace which the prophetic vision had foreseen turned out to be the *Pax Romana*. The *Pax Romana* was the peace brought by the Roman Empire and its armies. Athanasius, an Egyptian church leader, also wrote after the accession of Constantine to power. He referred likewise to the prophetic vision of Isaiah 2:1-4. He reported that the Greeks and barbarians had been torn by international and civil strife. When they became Christians, however, they had turned to peaceful ways.

But when they hear the teaching of Christ, straightway instead of fighting they turn to husbandry, and instead of arming their hands with weapons they raise them in prayer, and in a word, in place of fighting among themselves, henceforth they arm against the devil and against evil spirits.... They who become disciples of Christ, instead of warring with each other, stand arrayed against demons by their habits and virtuous actions. And they rout them and mock at their captain, the devil.[26]

Eusebius and Athanasius, like the writers before them, recognized that Christians were already participating in the kingdom of peace foretold by the prophets. However, the vision changed after Constantine became a Christian. Eusebius adapted the prophetic vision to the new situation by calling the empire an instrument of God. Athanasius limited the fulfillment of the prophecy to the sphere of spiritual warfare. He then could uphold the prophetic vision of messianic peace and let the followers of the Messiah fight the empire's wars.

By the time of Constantine, attitudes toward warfare were changing in the church. Yet the early church in general understood well that it was not the duty of Christians to fight in the wars of the empire. These early Christians interpreted the whole Bible in light of the law of love which they found most clearly revealed in the Gospels. They, therefore, could read the military narratives of the Old Testament without justifying Christian participation in war. By experience, they understood that their battle with evil was a real one. It was to be waged, however, on a different level, and with different weapons from the battles of the empire.

CHAPTER 3

Idolatry and Militarism

Some scholars suggest that early Christians opposed military service mainly because of the idolatry in the Roman army. This certainly was a problem for Christians living among pagans in the early centuries of the church. Paul wrote to the Christian community in Corinth about offerings made to idols. About 150 years later in North Africa, Tertullian wrote his treatise, *On Idolatry*. Idolatry was a problem for early Christians throughout the Roman Empire. The problem was even more acute for Christians who, for one reason or another, found themselves in the Roman army.

Thus, besides the brutality of bloodshed, the official idolatry in the Roman army also influenced Christians to refuse military service. The practice of emperor worship, a form of idolatry, had been evolving for centuries. Ancient Greeks tended to perceive gods as simply more-than-humans, or perhaps very great men. Quite naturally, this led them to consider the greatest of men as semi-gods. So, in practice, to consider an emperor divine was to simply acknowledge the extent and reality of his power.

This was idolatry, not speculation about divine and human nature as such. Originally, people were not required to worship the emperor, a practice that later varied from one part of the empire to another. Jews, for instance, were exempted from these ceremonies which clashed with their religious convictions. But as time went on, it became a crucial challenge to Christians.

The emperor's godlike nature was a political matter far more than it was a religious one. Emperor worship was not really concerned about the next world. Worshipers looked to the god-emperor for deliverance from this world's problems and dangers. So to the Romans, these ceremonies of emperor worship were certainly not mere empty forms. Ancient peoples believed that the head of the state held powers which he used for their common benefit.

The distaste for these imperial claims to divinity increased, however, as their ambitions grew more exaggerated. The early vague idea that emperors were gods because of their power gradually grew until they were almost considered biologically divine. However, in the year 291, a decisive change occurred. Emperors officially proclaimed themselves gods and sons of gods. Diocletian claimed to be the son of Jupiter. Maximilian pretended to be the son of Hercules. Constantine called himself the son of Apollo until he embraced Christianity.

Eventually, the army required an oath of loyalty to the emperor-gods. Christians, of course, opposed these outrageous claims of the emperors which made military service all the more objectionable to them.

Emperor worship in the Roman empire united the wide variety of ethnic and social groups who made up the population. Loyalty to the empire now took the form of emperor worship. At this point, however, Christians clashed with the claims of the empire. Christians were often reminded that they must choose between two kingdoms and two lords. The very titles which pagans applied to their rulers— such as *savior* and *lord*—were the ones which the Christians assigned to Jesus Christ. This fundamental conflict over who is lord was undoubtedly felt more acutely in the army than anywhere else. The army was closely bound to the emperor. Rituals of patriotic loyalty were repeated regularly in the practices of army religion. For Christians these were, of course, idolatry.

For this reason, army ceremonies often became the moment when Christians refused what they considered disloyalty to God. For this they suffered martyrdom. This kind of situation furnished the occasion for Tertullian's treatise *On The Crown*, written in 211. It is the first Christian writing dedicated totally to the question of Christians' participation in the army.

A Christian soldier had refused to conform to the requirements for a military ceremony. In order to receive a bonus granted by the emperor, the soldiers were ordered to present themselves in full military parade dress. It included a military crown made of laurel leaves. This dissenter, whose name we do not know, refused out of Christian conviction to wear his crown. Instead, he carried it in his hand. He was arrested for this offense against Roman army ritual and presumably executed.

In his treatise, Tertullian inferred that there were other Christians in the ranks at the time. But he accused them of pretending "that they could serve two masters." Tertullian also lamented that some Christians of his time would see this as "a mere matter of dress." Many were becoming lax in their Christian commitment in order to avoid persecution, he concluded.[27]

But more fundamental than the question of the military crown, and the idolatry it implied, was the question of

> whether military service is proper at all for Christians. What sense is there in discussing the merely accidental, when that on which it rests is to be condemned? . . . Shall it be held lawful to make an occupation of the sword, when the Lord proclaims that he who uses the sword shall perish by the sword? And shall the son of peace take part in the battle when it does not become him even to sue at law? And shall he apply the chain, and the prison, and the torture, and the punishment, who is not the avenger even of his own wrongs? . . . The very carrying of the Name over from the camp of light to the camp of darkness is a violation of it.[28]

Of course, Tertullian recognized that a soldier who was already in the Roman army might come to faith. And even though he cited the examples of the soldiers who came to John and the centurions who appear in the New Testament, Tertullian was quite emphatic.

> When a man has become a believer and faith has been sealed, there must be either an immediate abandonment of it, which has been the course with many, or all sorts of quibbling will have to be resorted to in order to avoid offending God, and that is not allowed even outside of military service. . . . Neither does military service hold out escape from punishment of sins. . . . Nowhere does the Christian change his character. . . . For if one is pressed to the offering of sacrifice and the sheer denial of Christ by the necessity of torture or of punishment . . . an excuse of this sort overturns the entire essence of our sacrament.[29]

When the unlawfulness of military life itself was recognized, the secondary question of the military crown and idolatrous ceremonies faded. By locating the problem in military life itself, rather than in the soldier's crown, Tertullian did not deny that idolatry was a problem. In reality, he set the problem in its full context. Idolatry does not consist simply of its ritual aspects. Military life itself is actually idolatrous because the emperor takes the role of Lord.

The Christian protest against idolatry was much broader than simply a question of sacrificing to the emperor. The following incident illustrates this fact.

In the year 259, the Spanish governor executed his bishop, Fructuosus, by burning him at the stake in the amphitheater in Tarragona. Before the matter of sacrificing to the emperor came up, the governor asked, "Were you aware of the emperor's orders?"

The bishop replied, "I do not know [his] orders. I am a Christian." When Fructuosus refused to participate in the idolatrous ritual, the governor exploded. "Who then will be obeyed, who will be honored, if people refuse to worship the gods and pay homage to the emperors?"[30]

Not all have recognized that military life is essentially religious in character. This was true of the Roman army, but it is also true to a certain extent of modern armies. Religion played a fundamental role in providing the cohesion and discipline which made the Roman army successful. Modern leaders continue to hold their military systems together and make them effective by a glue of ritual and tradition. These are not simply neutral components of the system.

Roman army life had a religious structure which affected

practically everything it did. It set the army's world apart from ordinary life and separated soldiers from civilians. Secure walls separated army camps from the outside world. The army provided models of what a good soldier should be. It taught respect for the gods and their representatives, the emperors. It offered a series of abstract deities who provided inspiration for army life, such as honor, virtue, loyalty, justice, and discipline. It also provided resources to help control natural fear of pain and death. Religious ceremonies and rituals provided distraction from fear and a basis for hope of victory.

Among the elements of the Roman army religion was respect for the legion's standards or symbols. Foremost among these was the eagle, symbolizing Jupiter who was thought to protect the empire. There were also ceremonies and offerings for personal protection from danger and for victories won.

The military oath, or sacramentum, was recited upon induction and repeated at regular intervals. It was an oath of absolute allegiance and unquestioning obedience to the emperor. Oaths could also be recited before the standards of the legion, since these represented military authority. In fact, there was even a sort of liturgical calendar which ordered the army religious festivals with their ceremonies and sacrifices.

Roman army religion functioned effectively to conserve ancient tradition. It also developed a nationalistic feeling in the army. Recruits came from all parts of the empire with a variety of religious orientations (including Christian). Army religion, therefore, stamped its imprint of Roman social, political, military, and moral values upon them.

Army religion did not end when Emperor Constantine

became a Christian early in the fourth century. Naturally, terminology changed and concepts varied. But army religion persisted with basically the same forms and functions as before.

Though the emperors tolerated Christianity and later established it, the idolatry of the army was still a problem for Christians. Idolatry was much bigger than the symbolic rituals themselves. It continued on the deeper level—one which Tertullian and other early Christians had so clearly perceived.

It was really still a question of "whether military service is proper at all for Christians." The army—and every other institution in which one cannot confess Jesus Christ as the only Lord—was, by its very nature, idolatrous. Service in the Roman army and service in the armies of modern nations are therefore alike in replacing God as king.

CHAPTER 4

The "Thundering" Legion

The first solid evidence of Christian soldiers in the army comes from about the year A.D. 173. Eusebius reported the incident in the year 323 in his *Church History*[31] However, the story may be more lengendary than factual.

Marcus Aurelius, the Roman emperor, was battling the Germans and the Sarmatians along the Danube River. In order to form his army, he had drawn soldiers from the Twelfth Legion based in the eastern part of the empire. According to the story, the soldiers, hard pressed in battle, were suffering from lack of water.

At this point, the legion prayed for deliverance with remarkable results. Immediately, a rainstorm blew up. Bolts of lightning put the enemy to flight, while the showers refreshed his troops. Following this miraculous deliverance in response to its prayers, the Legion was called "thundering" *(fulminatrix)*.

Apolinarius, bishop of Hierapolis, originally reported this story. Because he told it to Emperor Aurelius in his defense of Christians, many people consider it to be largely true. About 25 years later, Tertullian referred to this incident in his report to the emperor of his time, Septimus Severus. Some Christians may have been in the Twelfth Legion, since the troops came from a region where Christianity was strong. A secular historian of the period, Cassius Dio, tells another version of the story. He attributed the deliverance of the Twelfth Legion to the intervention of a roving Egyptian magician who was accompanying the emperor. The column erected in Rome in 176 in honor of Marcus Aurelius depicts three scenes of the rainstorm. Marcus himself is on his knees in prayer to Jupiter, the rain god. Jupiter is sending bolts of lightning upon the enemy and pouring out showers of refreshing rain upon the troops.

Disagreements in the story point to its legendary character. The Twelfth Legion, called *fulminata*, dates from the time of Augustus Caesar (28 B.C. to A.D. 14). It was thus so-named long before the miraculous deliverance reported by Eusebius. Rather than the *thundering* legion (*fulminatrix*), it was literally the *thunderstruck* legion (*fulminata*)—probably because lightning had struck the camp long before. Even if some Christians were in the legion, it is highly doubtful that the entire legion would have been Christians. These writers were trying to commend the Christians in the most favorable light to the imperial authorities. This was particularly true of Eusebius. Therefore, the story was likely embellished considerably.

At most, this story suggests the presence of Christians in the Roman army by this time. We can only speculate how they got there. Were they soldiers who had become Christians as a result of the church's missionary witness? Or were they already Christians, entering the army for one reason or another?

The presence of Christians in the army no doubt evolved

in this order. First, there were soldiers who became Christians and then there were Christians who became soldiers. This story and other warnings began to appear in Christian writings. They show that the participation of Christians in the Roman army was becoming a concern for the church.

However, the value of this evidence should not be overrated. In about the year 178 the pagan philosopher, Celsus, wrote a treatise called *True Discourse*. This is the oldest literary attack on Christianity of which we have knowledge. While Celsus praised some aspects of Christian doctrine and its high code of morals, he attacked other aspects of Christianity mercilessly. Among these was their nonconformity to the state. He claimed this undermined the state's strength and its will to resist its enemies.

Celsus urged Christians "to help the king with all our might . . . to labor with him in the maintenance of justice, to fight for him, and if he require it to fight under him, or lead an army with him."[32] Celsus was complaining that Christians were shirking their civic duties by refusing to take part in public or military life. Six decades later, Origen responded. He insisted that Christians who refuse enlistment in the army "are much more helpful to the kings than those who go into the field and fight for them."[33]

Thus, Celsus may have known of no Christians who were willing to perform military service. He wrote, "If all men were to do the same as you, there would be nothing to prevent [the king's] being left in utter solitude and desertion, and the forces of the empire would fall into the hands of the wildest and most lawless barbarians."[34]

CHAPTER 5

Tertullian
(A.D. c.160-c.230)

Tertullian, an early Christian writer, dealt most extensively with the question of early Christian attitudes toward warfare and military service. He was a native of Carthage in North Africa.

As a pagan, he studied law and probably moved to Rome. He became a Christian there when he was about 35 or 40 years old. He returned to his native city where he became a strong advocate of the Christian way. From the day of his conversion, he seems to have taken his commitment to Christ seriously.

In protest to the increasing moral laxity in the church, he joined the Montanist renewal movement for the last 15 years of his life. His writings span a period of about 20 years, from about 197 to 224. Throughout his career, he protested vigorously against the presence of Christians in the Roman army.

In 197 he wrote his *Apology* to refute the charge of antisocial behavior leveled against Christians. He said:

We are but of yesterday, and we have filled every place

among you—cities, islands, fortresses, towns, marketplaces, the very camp, tribes, companies, palace, senate, forum. We have left nothing to you but the temple of your gods. For what wars should we not be fit . . . if in our religion it were not counted better to be slain than to slay?[35]

So we sojourn with you in the world [rejecting] neither forum, nor shambles, nor bath, nor booth, nor worship, nor inn, nor weekly market, nor any other places of commerce. We sail with you, and *fight with you,* and till the ground with you.[36] (italics mine)

Writings such as these give us the most trustworthy evidence of the presence of Christians in the Roman army in the final decades of the second century. Clement of Alexandria, writing about the same time, spoke in similar terms.

Till the ground, we say, if you are a husbandman; but recognize God in your husbandry. Sail the sea, you who love seafaring; but ever call upon the heavenly Pilot. Were you a soldier on campaign when the knowledge of God laid hold on you? Then listen to the Commander who signals righteousness.[37]

Some have said that Clement thus authorized military service for Christians. However, the best interpretation probably points in the opposite direction. The soldier who has become a believer has passed from submission to a human leader to obedience to a truly righteous Leader. Although military service was a reality in the social context of Clement's time, he did not endorse it for Christians. Both Clement and Tertullian, however, noted that Christians served in the army in their time.

The writings of the early church leaders are not always

clear about the relationship between church and society. The church is, of course, based on love and peace, and society is based ultimately on military power. Tertullian, however, was clear in his opposition to violence. The following excerpt taken from his *On Idolatry*, written in about the year 211, sets forth clearly his position.

> But now the question is whether a believer can become a soldier and whether a soldier can be admitted into the faith even if he is a member only of the rank and file who are not required to take part in sacrifice or capital punishment. There can be no compatibility between the divine and the human sacrament [i.e., the military oath], the standard of Christ, and the standard of the devil, the camp of light and the camp of darkness. One soul cannot serve two masters— God and Caesar. Moses, to be sure, carried a rod; Aaron wore a military belt, and John is girt with leather [i.e., like a soldier]; and if you really want to play around with the subject, Joshua, the son of Nun, led an army and people waged war. But how will a Christian man go to war? Indeed, how will he serve in peacetime without a sword which the Lord has taken away? For even if soldiers came to John and received advice on how to act, and even a centurion became a believer, the Lord in subsequently disarming Peter disarmed every soldier. No uniform is lawful among us if it is designated for an unlawful action.[38]

Tertullian opposed military service for religious reasons because of its idolatrous sacrifice. He opposed it for ethical reasons because of its capital punishment. He also opposed it because it was part of a system at war against God—a "camp of darkness." Many have argued that the early Christians opposed the military because they did not want to participate in the army's idolatry. While this was an important consideration for this opposition, it was not the only or most important reason. The church's opposition to militarism was also ethical. Even more, it was systematic. The ethical bases for Tertullian's rejection of militarism are especially clear in his sensitivity toward human life. This concern is both stated and implied in his writings.

Tertullian believed humans are the unique center of God's creation—that they bear the divine image.[39] Therefore, a person's life is precious. The humblest person among the living is worth more than the greatest of the dead.[40]

The bloody games held by the Romans in Jupiter's honor were especially revolting to Tertullian. Though it was criminals who were given to the beasts, these spectacles were utterly shameful, he said. In all cases, taking human life was murder.[41] Tertullian insisted that Christians are all brothers and sisters, not merely among themselves, but also among the rest of humanity. Therefore, to act in an unbrotherly way toward anyone was to run the risk of losing one's own humanity.[42]

This reality of being a member of the whole human family was a part of Tertullian's argument against military service. In the following quotation, he shows the hollowness of military victory and its effect on those who fight.

> Is the laurel of the triumph made of leaves, or of corpses? Is it adorned with ribbons, or with tombs? Is it bedewed with ointments, or with the tears of wives and mothers? It may be of some Christians too; for Christ is also among the barbarians. Has not he who has carried [a crown for] this cause on his head, fought against himself?[43]

Killing any person, Tertullian argued, is a devil-inspired crime against God. Christians reject abortion and capital punishment for the same reason. Even though the condemned may be criminals, they are still persons. Tertullian observed the irony of preserving the life of the fetus or of the condemned murderer, only to sacrifice these lives in warfare.[45] He knew that Christians would suffer because they opposed such violence. But this self-sacrifice, required of all who participate in the "war of the Lamb," leads to truth and eternal life.[46]

CHAPTER 6

Origen
(A.D. c.185-c.254)

Origen, a strong Christian leader from Alexandria, lived and worked in Palestine during the last 24 years of his life. His mother saved him from martyrdom as a youth when she hid his clothing to prevent him from leaving the house. Near the end of his life, he was imprisoned and tortured. He survived this only a few years.

There was certainly no gap between Origen's theology and his practice. He was an outstanding teacher and one of the most outspoken advocates of peace and nonviolence in the early church.

As we noted before, Origen was among the early Christian writers who affirmed the vision of Isaiah 2:1-4. Origen saw God's kingdom on earth being fulfilled through the emergence of a community of peace led by the Messiah. He told Celsus, the pagan critic of the early Christian movement, that Christians are by nature peace-loving people. Jesus had absolutely forbidden the killing of other human beings.

The Christian Lawgiver . . . nowhere teaches that it is right for his own disciples to offer violence to anyone, however wicked.... Christians ... were taught not to avenge themselves upon their enemies.[47]

Celsus complained that the Christians were shirking their civic duties by refusing public life and military service. The response which follows represents Origen's thinking on this theme.

Celsus urges us "to help the king with all our might, and to labor with him in the maintenance of justice, to fight for him; and if he requires it, to fight under him, or lead an army along with him." To this, our answer is that we do, when the occasion requires, give help to kings, and so to say, a divine help "putting on the whole armor of God." And we do this in obedience to the injunction of the apostle, "I exhort, therefore, that first of all supplication, prayers, intercessions, and giving of thanks be made for all men; for kings and for all that are in authority."

And the more anyone excels in piety, the more effective help does he render to kings, even more than is given by soldiers, who go forth to fight and slay as many of the enemy as they can.... And even when war is upon you, you never enlist the priests in the army. If that then is a laudable custom, how much more so that while others are engaged in battle, these too should engage as the priests and ministers of God, keeping their hands pure and wrestling in prayers to God in behalf of those who are fighting in a righteous cause, and for the king who reigns righteously, that whatever is opposed to those who act righteously may be destroyed!"

And we by our prayer vanquish all demons who stir up war

and lead to the violation of oaths and disturb the peace. We in this way are much more helpful to the kings than those who go into the field to fight for them. And we do take our part in public affairs, when along with the righteous prayers we join self-denying exercises and meditations, which teach us to despise pleasures and not to be led away by them. And none fight better for the king than we do. We do not indeed fight under him, although he require it; but we fight on his behalf, forming a special army—an army of piety—by offering our prayers to God.[48]

Origen's reply to Celsus brings together some of the attitudes of the early church toward war. First, he neither denied nor modified Celsus' observation that Christians refuse to participate in wars. Origen had traveled widely in the church and knew the early Christian movement well. Writing about 250, he probably knew of rare cases of Christians in the Roman army. He spoke for a broad sector of the church, however, when he defended the rightness of the early Christian opposition to warfare.

Second, Origen responded directly to Celsus' charge of irrelevance. He insisted that the church can make its best contribution to society by simply and fully being the church. This included resistance to the pressures to participate in the violence used to establish order within society. It also suggested the existence of a community characterized by righteous living and internal discipline.

Third, Origen also called for participation in combat—but at a different level. Early Christians shared the conviction that social evil is essentially a demonic reality. Therefore, one must combat evil through the spiritual resources of prayer and nonviolent resistance. However, this spiritual warfare is not in place of social responsibility and relationships marked by justice among Christians. Rather, it is the alternative to the physical violence of warfare.

Origen no doubt did not intend to respond to all objections in this brief passage. One can infer from his statement, of course, that it is the will of God for the state to resort to violence to maintain a just social order. The point is that Origen forbids Christians to participate in such violence. He probably believed that God wills for all humanity to submit to God's rule, thereby making violence unnecessary. Origen did not address whether it was right to use violence before all accepted God's reign.

Finally, there is the reference to Christians as priests. Through their purity and prayers to God, they strive "for those who fight in a righteous cause." Some have seen this as an admission that the wars of the emperor are just and necessary, and especially in the case of a good emperor. After the emperor became a "Christian," Christians began to justify participation in those wars which were considered just.

However, Origen was not responsible for this conclusion. He was responding to Celsus who considered the cause of the pagan emperor righteous. Origen said that Christians—by their nonviolence and their prayers— contribute to the common welfare under pagan emperors.

CHAPTER 7

The Apostolic Tradition of Hippolytus (A.D. c.170-c.236)

Hippolytus was an important teacher in the church in Rome. He, like his contemporary Tertullian, was a strong advocate of ethical seriousness in the church. He resisted idolatrous practices and other false values in Roman society which more and more Christians were accepting. He even appears to have disagreed with the Roman church in his opposition to two of the bishops and their teachings. Later, the emperor Maximilian banished him, together with Pope Pontianus.

The *Apostolic Tradition* was one of the earliest and most important of the ancient Christian church orders. Many believe that Hippolytus wrote it, since its contents are compatible with what we know about his attitude in general. The *Apostolic Tradition* seems to have expressed an early Christian consensus. It served as a basis for other church orders which continued to appear in other parts of the empire as much as two centuries later. It represents the teaching of the church at Rome around the year A. D. 200.

Several articles in the document list occupations or professions which were forbidden for candidates for church membership. These include brothel keepers, actors, participants in the circus or in gladiatorial combat, and makers and keepers of idols. Also forbidden were male and female prostitutes, magicians, astrologers, and all others who persisted in some form of immorality. Three articles address the question of the church's attitude toward warfare.

> 17) A soldier who is of inferior rank shall not kill anyone. If ordered to, he shall not carry out the order, nor shall he take the oath. If he does not accept this, let him be dismissed.
>
> 18) Anyone who has the power of the sword or the magistrate of a city who wears purple, let him give it up or be dismissed.
>
> 19) The catechumen or believers who wish to become soldiers shall be dismissed because they have despised God.[49]

In addition to immorality and magic, the *Apostolic Tradition* denounces idolatry and violence that causes death. In fact, these two were linked together both in circus spectacles and the army. There was a relationship between the games of the gladiators and war. In peacetime, the Romans kept up the military spirit with these murderous shows in the arena.

Some suggest that the prohibition of killing in the *Apostolic Tradition* refers to the execution of criminals in the arena (capital punishment). The context seems to point in this direction more than toward the taking of life in warfare. However, this prohibition undoubtedly applies to all killing.

Participation in the Roman army apparently did not always involve combat or the carrying out of punishments. Other functions of the army included road maintenance, mail services, guard duty, and other forms of civil service. Therefore, soldiers who refused to kill and to take the military oath might remain in the army. To take the military oath, however, was more than simply going through an induction ceremony. The military oath was a regular feature of army life, being administered at least three times a year. It was at the core a part of the idolatrous rituals of Roman militarism. Article 17 of the *Apostolic Tradition* appears to contemplate the situation of a soldier who has become a believer. Article 19, however, forbids believers to become soldiers.

Church leaders recognized that Christians should not have been serving in the army, but they were. These persons were ordered not to kill, but sometimes they did. The church condemned such conduct, and offenders could be readmitted to fellowship only by repenting of their sin.

Military violence was forbidden for Christians. Furthermore, legal civil violence, such as that which a magistrate might order inflicted upon a person, was also prohibited for Christians.

These prohibitions of military service continued for more than two centuries in church orders drawn up in Ethiopia, Syria, and Egypt. After Constantine embraced Christianity, believers began to accommodate their practices to the new political situation. Even so, the earlier prohibitions of military service and killing continued to appear in the church orders of the period. However, as time went on, exceptions were added.

CHAPTER 8

Military Martyrs

Marinus

As the number of Christians in the Roman army slowly increased, the number who suffered a martyr's death also increased.

Eusebius reports the martyrdom of Marinus from Caesarea in Palestine around the year 260. He was a member of an illustrious and wealthy family. A soldier in the Roman army, he had been honored for his service and had been recommended for the rank of centurion. At one point, another candidate for promotion accused Marinus of being a Christian who would not sacrifice to the emperor. Such refusal would disqualify him for the post.

Confronted with this charge, Marinus readily admitted to being a Christian. His superior granted him a three-hour recess to reconsider the matter of his loyalty. During this recess, his bishop brought him to the local church and placed him before the altar. Pointing to the soldier's sword, the bishop offered Marinus a choice between his weapon and the copy of the Gospels which he held in his hand. According to the story, Marinus immediately chose the Gospels and willingly faced martyrdom.[50]

Eusebius' report of this incident no doubt contains legendary elements. It does show that by this time some soldiers were becoming Christians. It also shows that the church often forced them to decide between two loyalties. They could either participate in the idolatry of the Roman army or they could become martyrs for Christ themselves. Most of the accounts of soldier martyrs come from the period of intense persecution during the reign of Diocletian (284-305). Eusebius, a contemporary of these events, noted that the persecution began with the Christians in the army. According to his report, there must have been a considerable number of Christians in the Roman army by this time.[51]

Maximilian

On March 12, 295, Maximilian refused induction into the Roman army in North Africa for reasons of conscience. According to the *Acts* of the trial,[52] Maximilian, a 21-year-old youth, was summoned to the forum together with his father. When the proconsul asked the youth's name before his induction, Maximilian replied, "But why do you wish to know my name? I cannot serve because I am a Christian."

The official persisted, "Get him ready." As the process began, Maximilian again replied, "I cannot serve. I cannot commit a sin. I am a Christian." Even so, he was measured and the proconsul ordered that he be given the military seal. Still resisting, Maximilian replied once more, "I will not do it! I cannot serve!"

"Serve, or you will die!" the proconsul threatened.

"I shall not serve," replied Maximilian. "You may cut off my head. I will not serve this world, but only my God."

After attempting another ruse to convince him, the proconsul ordered, "Agree to serve and receive the military seal."

"I will not accept the seal," answered Maximilian. "I already have the seal of Christ." Resisting further threats, he added, "I will not accept the seal of this world. If you give it to me, I shall break it—I am a Christian! I cannot wear a piece of lead around my neck after I have received the saving sign of Jesus Christ my Lord!"

After adding further threats and orders to no avail, the proconsul said, "There are [other] soldiers who are Christians, and they serve."

To this Maximilian responded, "They know what is best for them. But I am a Christian, and I cannot do wrong."

The official then added, "What wrong do they commit who serve in the army?"

Maximilian replied quite simply, "Why, you know what they do!"

Additional threats were of no avail, and Maximilian was sentenced to die by the sword. The last two sentences are missing in some manuscripts of the *Acts* of the trial. They contain a clear declaration by Maximilian against serving in the Roman army. Maximilian died for his conviction. Ironically, the church came to respect him as a martyr but rejected his position in its official moral teaching.

Several things stand out in this story. First, Maximilian insisted from the start that he was refusing induction into the Roman army because as a Christian he could not serve as a soldier (*militare*). Many have held that his objection to military service came from his rejection of idolatry. One engaged in such idolatry by accepting the seal of the emperor and the practices of the army. However, the question of sacrifice (either to the emperor or to idols) was not mentioned by either party in the trial. Maximilian expressed his objection to military service before the matter of accepting the seal was introduced.

Furthermore, the idolatry implied in the acceptance of the seal and in Roman army life was far more than a matter of ritual. He refused the seal because he had already received the seal of Christ. The contrast was between "the seal of this world" and the "saving sign of Jesus Christ ... whom all we Christians serve; we follow him as the Prince of Life." So rather than just a question of formal idolatrous practices, it was a matter of refusing an entire system of idolatrous loyalties. The Roman army was a part of this system. This idea of two kingdoms marked by loyalty to two lords had prevailed since New Testament times.

Maximilian was buried next to Cyprian's grave in Carthage. Thus, this "conscientious objector" to Roman militarism was honored by burying him near the grave of Cyprian, the disciple of Tertullian. Cyprian himself was an outspoken advocate of peace and a severe critic of military service.

Marcellus

Marcellus was a centurion in the Seventh Legion of the Roman army stationed in Spain. He was arrested in 298 for throwing down his belt and sword in front of the flag of the empire during a military parade. Brought before the governor, Marcellus declared, "I answered publicly and ... confessed that I was a Christian and ... could not fight by any other oath, but solely for the Lord Christ Jesus."

Because the offense of Marcellus was so grave, his case went to a superior court located across the Straits of Gibraltar in Tangier. When the Roman prefect there questioned him, Marcellus confessed that he had indeed thrown down his weapons. "For it is not fitting that a Christian, who fights for Christ his Lord, should be a soldier according to the brutalities of this world."[53] He was then condemned to execution by the sword.

The story of Marcellus also contributes to our understanding of the attitude of early Christians toward military service. Marcellus had been a soldier long enough to have risen to the rank of centurion of the first cohort of the Seventh Legion based in Spain. We do not know when Marcellus became a Christian. However, Marcellus found the conflict of loyalties disturbing. Even though he was a soldier, he was now first and foremost a Christian.

The belt and sword were symbols of Roman military life. Throwing them to the ground, therefore, was a symbolic gesture of protest to imperial and army religion. But beyond the rejection of these idolatrous rituals was the underlying concept of citizenship in another kingdom and service under a different lord. Marcellus had come to the conviction that to serve in the Roman army was to "be a soldier according to the brutalities of this world." As a soldier of Jesus Christ, he could not in good conscience continue in the legions of Caesar.

Julius

The record of Julius' martyrdom contains a number of legendary features. Although a mixture of legend and fact, the story is worth noting.

A veteran in the Roman army, Julius had served 27 years by the time of his execution in the year 303. He had refused to offer the symbolic incense to the gods, as ordered by the emperors. In his defense, Julius seems to have remained proud of his service record. The Roman prefect who judged his case offered a number of ruses by which Julius might have saved his life and soothed the judge's conscience. However, Julius was not willing to compromise his integrity merely to avoid execution.

The idolatrous rituals of the Roman army became the point at which Julius took his stand of protest. In his defense before the magistrate he cited his good conduct in the army as evidence of his personal integrity. However, he apparently had second thoughts about his long period of military service. "It appears that I made a mistake in serving in that worthless army [*vana militia*]."[54] Julius understood clearly the difference between the laws of the empire and God's law. For him, God's law alone carried absolute authority.

Pachomius (c. 290-346)

Pachomius and his companions were not actually military martyrs in the narrow sense of the term. However, through their imprisonment, they bore witness to the early Christian opposition to service in the Roman army. While some hold that Pachomius served in the Roman army, it is difficult to separate facts from legend. The facts, however, confirm the following story.

Constantine, at the beginning of his reign, waged war against his rivals for power. To meet this crisis, he ordered that soldiers be recruited and an army prepared for battle.

Pachomius, a young pagan 20 years old then, was recruited and embarked with a group of young Christian men from upper Egypt. For some reason, possibly as deserters, they were all imprisoned in Thebes without ever leaving Egypt. During their imprisonment, members of the local Christian congregation generously supported them. Meanwhile, the triumph of Constantine over his rivals permitted him to order the release of recruits throughout the empire. At that point, Pachomius and his friends were also released and joyfully returned to their homes.

These Christian recruits had spent the entire period of their service in chains. Their church apparently thought that their situation was normal for Christians. This story continued to be narrated even after the church, under Constantine, began to accept military service. Apparently these imprisoned recruits were protesting in the spirit of the *Apostolic Tradition* their forced involvement in the Roman army. The protest continued in the Egyptian church orders of this period. The contact of Pachomius with this group of Christian recruits may have led to his conversion in prison.

Immediately following his liberation from prison, Pachomius requested baptism. Later, he became the founder of a nonviolent Christian movement in Egypt which developed into communal monasticism.

Martin of Tours (c. 316-397)

As the dates above show, the life of Martin of Tours falls within the Constantinian era. In this era, Christianity was first tolerated. Later it was favored, and finally it was established as the only lawful religion in the empire. Therefore, Martin's refusal to continue in the Roman army is all the more noteworthy. The resistance of the early church to military service in the era of persecution was continued by Martin in the new era of church peace.

Martin's pagan father was a military tribune. Because an imperial edict required the enlistment of veterans' sons, Martin was forced to become a soldier. In fact, he was brought in chains to take the military oath. During this time, Martin was a convert receiving instruction in the Christian way. Shortly afterwards, he was baptized at the age of 18.

Following his baptism, he continued in the army in "a purely nominal fashion only." Sources do not agree on just how long this nominal service in the army lasted. Finally, Martin requested release from military service. "Hitherto," he said, "I have served you as a soldier. Allow me now to become a soldier of God. Let the man who is to serve you receive your *donative* [commission]. I am a soldier of Christ. It is not lawful for me to fight."[55]

Among the accusations against Martin was the charge of cowardice. So Martin asked that on the following day he be allowed to stand unarmed in front of the line of battle. The next day the barbarian troops surrendered without a fight. Martin's biographer later wrote about this event.

> Yet that his blessed eyes might not be pained by witnessing the death of others, he removed all necessity for fighting. For Christ did not require . . . any other victory in behalf of his own soldier, than that the enemy [be] subdued without bloodshed.[56]

By this time, the emperors were Christians and Christianity was tolerated and even favored in the empire. Therefore, Martin's refusal to serve in the army was not due primarily to the idolatrous practices of military life. (At least not in their ritual forms.)The army, as well as other institutions, had been depaganized, at least in theory. It also seems that Martin wanted Rome to keep control over the enemies of the empire. However, it was the shedding of blood which Martin considered to be an intolerable evil.

In Martin's experience, we note again a theme which strongly influenced Christians throughout the early history of the church. That is, the Christian is a soldier of Christ. One's loyalty to the kingdom in which Christ is Lord surpasses all other loyalties.

What we know of Martin's life after his refusal to continue in the Roman army is consistent with his objection to military service. In 360, he started the first monastic community in France. Twelve years later he became bishop of Tours. He strongly opposed the violence and persecution which the church inflicted against Priscillian and his followers in Spain.

According to Sulpicius Severus, a younger contemporary and biographer, Martin never returned evil for evil. No one ever saw him angry, and his heart was full of piety, peace, and compassion.

CHAPTER 9

An Early Christian Alternative to Warfare

Faced with violent suffering, early Christians chose a remarkable alternative to violence. The early church leaders who wrote in Latin called this attitude *patientia*. Although the English word *patience* is derived from this term, it does not express fully the word's meaning. *Patientia* means the steadfast endurance to resist evil without doing violence to the evildoer. This concept appears in the New Testament. There it carries the sense of firm and enduring resistance to the evil and violent pressures of injustice and persecution. This is undoubtedly the sense of the term translated *endurance* in Revelation 13:10 and 14:12, for example.

Even in defense of the highest of values, the early church rejected the killing of one human being by another. The Christians believed such violence totally opposed the foundations of Christian faith. They knew by experience that the Spirit of Christ was not the same spirit which inspired social relationships in their pagan society. This power of love in their midst freed them from the need to rely on raw force. "Every word which [goes] out of your mouth in faith and love shall tend to bring conversion and hope to many."[57]

They themselves had experienced the presence of God's kingdom marked by the power of love. They trusted both the providence and the protection of God for their life and survival in this world. This freed them from the need to use violence to protect and provide for themselves. Though they lived in a violent society, they endured the evils of injustice and persecution, confident of their part in the victory of the Lamb. We need not look far to discover the source of this conviction. It contrasted sharply with the predominant values of Greek and Roman societies. Among the ancient Greeks and Romans, the Christian understanding of *patientia* was anything but a virtue. They saw it as a mark of shame and a sign of a slave. The earliest Christian writings agree that the source of this vision flows from the spirit and life and teachings of Jesus. *The Teaching of the Twelve Apostles*, dating from about A.D. 115, recognized two fundamentally different principles of social organization. One is the way of life. The other is death.

Jesus' teachings in Matthew 5:38-48 describe human relationships which lead to life. The revolutionary power of this vision is summed up in the phrase: "Love those who hate you and you will no longer have an enemy."[58] At the center of this vision is the command to love God and the neighbor as oneself. For additional clarity, the second command is stated, "Thou shalt not kill." And this included specifically the prohibition of abortion and infanticide. All of these forms of murder were relatively common in pagan society of the first century.

Clement of Rome wrote near the end of the first century. He warned against the temptation to depend on the power of superior intelligence, force, and wealth. The alternative to these sources of power is found in "the words of the Lord Jesus which he spake teaching us meekness and long-suffering [*patientia*]."[59]

Ignatius, the bishop of Antioch, wrote the following words shortly after the turn of the first century. He said, "Nothing is more precious than peace by which all war, both in heaven and on earth, is brought to an end."[60] In another context, Ignatius wrote that it is "meekness by which the prince of this world is destroyed."[61]

This understanding of peace has little in common with the peace which Augustine described a little more than three centuries later. Augustine, speaking for the church after Constantine, admitted that in his time people saw peace as an inward and future reality. Peace among peoples and nations needed to be established through warfare. In contrast, the peace of which Ignatius wrote is dynamic and powerful—capable of overcoming the violence of both humans and demons.

Aristides described the life of the Christians of his time in about 125. He said,

> What they do not want others to do to them they do not do to others. They exhort those who harm them and try to turn them into friends. They go out of the way to do good to their enemies. They are meek and humble.... They are willing to give their lives for the cause of Christ, since they steadfastly obey his commandments.[62]

In his *First Apology*, written about 155, Justin Martyr

defended the Christians to the Roman emperor Antonius and his sons. He wrote,

> We who hated and destroyed one another, and on account of their different manners would not live with men of a different tribe, now, since the coming of Christ, live familiarly with them. [We] pray for our enemies and endeavor to persuade those who hate us unjustly to live conformably to the good precepts of Christ.[63]

After citing Jesus' teaching recorded in Matthew 5:11, 16, 39-41, Justin said more.

> For we ought not to strive; neither has he desired us to be imitators of wicked men, but he has exhorted us to lead all men by patience and gentleness from shame and the love of evil.[64]

Athenagoras addressed his *Plea for the Christians* to the Roman Emperor Marcus Aurelius in about 177. He insisted that Christians are different because they have been taught by God himself.

In response to the question, "What are these teachings which nurture us?" he answered by citing Matthew 5:44-45. Then he continued.

> Among us you will find uneducated persons, artisans, and old women.... They are unable in words to prove the benefit of our doctrine, yet by their deeds [they] exhibit the benefit arising from their persuasion of its truth; they do not rehearse speeches but exhibit good works; when struck, they do not strike again; when robbed, they do not go to law; they give to those that ask of them, and love their neighbors as themselves.[65]

Tertullian later developed this Christian idea of steadfast endurance—or nonviolent resistance to evil—in a more systematic way. The principle, of course, applies to all areas of social relationships. It addresses the problem of behavior toward both personal and national enemies. The commitment of Christians to their Lord is absolute. Therefore, they are by definition children of peace.

This places both collective and personal violence outside the orbit of the Christian's activity. As individuals, they neither sued at law nor tried to avenge the personal wrongs committed against them. As a group, they placed military service, war, and the administration of legal justice outside the realm of acceptable activity for Christians. Tertullian wrote his *Apology* on behalf of the Christians. In it he suggested that had they been willing to defend themselves with weapons, their numbers may well have ensured their victory. But he noted that Christians are given more liberty to be killed than to kill.[66]

In fact, earlier in the same treatise, Tertullian had briefly mentioned a strategy which is strikingly similar to some modern methods of nonviolent resistance.

> Why—without taking up arms, without rebellion, simply by standing aside, by mere ill-natured separation—we could have fought you! For if so vast a mass of people as we had broken away from you and removed to some recess of the world apart, the mere loss of so many citizens of whatever sort would have brought a blush to your rule! Yes, that it would, and punished you too by sheer desertion! Beyond doubt, you would have shuddered at your solitude, at the silence in the world, the stupor as it were of a dead globe. You would have had to look about for a people to rule![67]

But early Christians did not employ this strategy, even if it was nonviolent. They believed that the best contribution the church could make to society was to be simply and truly the community of Jesus. An earlier advocate of the Christians had written in his *Epistle to Diognetus* that Christians are, in effect, the soul which enables society to survive.

> Christians are not distinguished from their fellow humans by nationality, language, or customs.... However, they exhibit a particular kind of conduct which is admirable and, according to general opinion, surprising.... They obey the established laws; but in their living, they surpass them by far. They show love to all, but everyone persecutes them.... They are cursed, but in this, they are declared righteous. They are reviled, but they in turn bless.... To state the matter briefly, as the soul is to the body, so are Christians in the world.... It is they who hold the world together.[68]

Early Christians were determined to live according to the values they had learned from Jesus and from the community which had formed around him. In effect, they were a contrast society created and nurtured by a force more powerful than that which sustained traditional society. They steadfastly resisted evil, while refusing to resist evil persons with their weapons of violence. This kind of endurance pointed toward God's future reign of righteousness. Violent persons would eventually be overcome by this revolutionary movement which rejected the impure means of violence.

In his written account to Scapula, the Roman proconsul,

Tertullian recalled an example of nonviolent witness. In Asia, under Arrius Antonius, Christians had responded to persecution by going as a group to the tribunal to be condemned. This unexpected support of the accused person and noteworthy commitment to witness embarrassed and confused the persecutor.

Tertullian then put the question to Scapula. What would he do if "thousands of those under his administration, men and women of all ages and conditions, were to come and offer themselves voluntarily for martyrdom?" Others beside Tertullian noted that the more Christians suffered with steadfast endurance, the more the movement grew. In a profound sense, the innocent suffering of Christians is an act of self-defense rooted in faith. In the conclusion of his treatise to Scapula, Tertullian noted that

> We have no master but God. He is before you, and cannot be hidden from you, but to him you can do no injury. But whom you regard as masters are only men, and one day they themselves must die. Yet still this community will be undying, for be assured that just in the time of its seeming overthrow, it is built up into greater power. For all who witness the noble patience of its martyrs are struck with misgivings, are inflamed with desire to examine into the matter in question; and as soon as they come to know the truth, they straightway enroll themselves as its disciples.[69]

Early in his career as a Christian writer, Tertullian wrote an account entitled *De Patientia*. He insisted that steadfast endurance is the only valid response for Christians in the face of violence. This vision, he declared, was not the product of philosophical wisdom nor the prudence of practical persons. Its origin was divine.[70]

From God's perspective, no real difference exists between an aggressor and a person who seeks vengeance. Even if the aggressor is the first to do evil, the reaction of the latter is similar and equally wrong before God. Christians, therefore, are not to return evil for evil. They should sacrifice their honor by surrendering the right to defend themselves according to natural inclination.[71] Not even the Christian faith needed to be defended by violent means, much less other less important causes.

This nonviolent stance was rooted in the very nature of God's grace. Jesus Christ himself was the originator and the Lord of *patientia*. He had taught his disciples that they could be children of their heavenly Father insofar as they were obedient to his commandment of *patientia*. "The universal rule of patience is contained in this essential commandment: We may not do evil even when it might seem justifiable."[72]

Origen, who wrote about 50 years after Tertullian, responded to the charge that the Christian movement was the result of a violent revolution:

> If a revolt had led to the formation of the Christian commonwealth ... the Christian Lawgiver would not have altogether forbidden the putting of men to death; and yet he nowhere teaches that it is right for his own disciples to offer violence to anyone, however wicked. For he did not deem it in keeping with such laws as his, which were derived from a divine source, to allow the killing of any individual whatever. Nor would the Christians, had they owed their origin to a rebellion, have adopted laws of so exceedingly mild a character as not to allow them, when it was their fate to be slain as sheep, on any occasion to resist

> their persecutors. . . . Because they were taught not to
> avenge themselves upon their enemies . . . and because
> they would not, although able, have made war even if they
> had received authority to do so.[73]

Origen insisted that Jesus did not need to use the
methods of violence as the people of God had under the
old covenant. The force of Christ's teaching was powerful
enough to spread the Word everywhere.[74]

Although emperors and rulers tried to humiliate Christians by persecution, their endurance demonstrated God's
grace among them. These Christians did not intentionally
expose themselves to beatings, tortures, and death. They
believed, however, that the violence of vengeance and the
unfaithfulness of idolatry were too high a price to pay for
relief.

Cyprian, the North African bishop who followed
Tertullian, also wrote a tract entitled *De Bono Patientiae*.
He basically shared Tertullian's vision of Christian nonviolence. Human *patientia* is rooted in the *patientia* of God
whose loving forebearance toward rebellious humanity is
noteworthy. However, the words and deeds of Jesus
manifest the meaning of *patientia* with even more clarity.
Cyprian cited Matthew 5:43-48 as a concrete example of
Jesus' teaching on *patientia*. His suffering on the cross was
the prime example of Jesus' steadfast endurance. It is
precisely this nonviolent endurance of Jesus which Christians are to imitate.[75]

Cyprian also wrote:

> But patience, beloved brethren, not only keeps watch over
> what is good, but it also repels what is evil. In harmony with
> the Holy Spirit, and associated with what is heavenly and

divine, it struggles with the defense of its own strength against the deeds of the flesh. . . . It is patience . . . which directs our doing, that we may hold fast the way of Christ which we walk by His patience. It is this that makes us to persevere as sons of God while we imitate our Father's patience.[76]

Cyprian addressed the following words to Demetrianus, a Roman official probably in charge of passing judgment against Christians.

None of us, when he is apprehended, makes resistance, nor avenges himself against your unrighteous violence, although our people are numerous and plentiful. . . . We may not hate, and we please God more by rendering no return for wrong. . . . We repay kindness for your hatred.[77]

Lactantius, at 60 years of age, became a Christian around the year 300. He had been a teacher of rhetoric before his conversion. In his writings, he attempted to commend Christianity to the thinking people of his time. As others before him had done, he also extolled *patientia* as the greatest of Christian virtues. To return an injury, he wrote, is to imitate the evil of the person who does violence.[78] Later, he expanded this concept.

It is the part of a wise and excellent man not to wish to remove his adversary, which cannot be done without guilt and danger, but to put an end to the contest itself, which may be done with advantage and with justice. Therefore, patience is to be regarded as a very great virtue . . . If when provoked by injury, he has begun to follow up his assailant with violence, he is overcome. But if he shall have repressed that emotion by reasoning, he altogether has command over himself; he is able to rule himself. And this restraining of oneself is rightly named patience, which single virtue is opposed to all vices and affections.[79]

Augustine was largely responsible for developing the classic just war theory. It limited Christian participation in warfare to certain justifiable situations. Even he, however, wrote an entire treatise on the theme of *patientia*. His definition of the patient person is a masterpiece. Such a person "prefers to endure evil so as not to commit it, rather than to commit evil so as not to endure it."[80]

The church leaders whose writings we have reviewed were not naive. They knew that the exercise of Christian *patientia* would not always end in immediate victory with a minimum of suffering. The price was often the martyrdom of the person who steadfastly persevered. Occasionally, responses of gentleness and steadfastness, far from calming evil tempers, enraged them even more.

This points up the double meaning which the cross of Christ has for Christians. It shows first the cruel price which they sometimes need to pay in order to follow their Lord. However, the cross of Christ also reminds us that the most complete defeat can also in the end lead to the only true victory.

CHAPTER 10

Constantine's Shift

Constantine (306-337) gained power in the Roman Empire during the second decade of the fourth century. His military skill and political wisdom permitted him to triumph over his opponents in the struggle for power.

Christians have interpreted his rise to power in widely different ways. Some have viewed it as a key event in the establishing of God's reign on earth. Others have related it directly to the "fall of the church." Obviously, neither of these descriptions accurately reflects the changes brought about in the church by Constantine's embrace of Christianity.

Eusebius, a bishop of the church in Caesarea from about 315, was the leading advocate of the first of these interpretations. In his *Church History*, completed in 323, Eusebius sought to interpret the history of the Roman Empire from a Christian point of view. According to Eusebius, the empire was successful because Christ was born during the reign of the Emperor Octavian. The beginning of the empire and the birth of Christ, therefore, coincided, bringing in a new age of salvation. Eusebius described

Constantine as God's agent in restoring the fortunes of Christians within the empire, as well as reestablishing historic Roman liberty. In the view of Eusebius, Constantine was victorius in the violent power struggle with his adversaries because of divine assistance.[81]

The *Pax Romana* (Roman Peace), described in glowing terms by Eusebius, was the result of divine intervention.[82] A series of imperial decrees emerged from Constantine's growing alliance with the church. In the year 311, Constantine officially tolerated Christian faith and worship. In 313 he decreed religious freedom and the restoration of previously confiscated church properties.[83] He offered monetary grants to the clergy, who were also exempted from all political or civic responsibilities.[84]

Although Christianity was not made the official religion until about 380, Eusebius generously praised the empire for the benefits which had fallen upon the church. Eusebius concluded his *Church History* with optimism. He was certain God's reign had been universally established in the context of a universal empire.[85]

On the other hand, some historians have maintained that Eusebius did not clearly see Constantine's relationship to the church. The so-called conversion of Constantine did not really bring a substantial change. While he was kind toward Christians, Constantine was at the same time protecting and supporting pagan religion. Christian emperors retained the title of *Pontifex Maximus* (pagan high priest) until the year 379. Between 310-326, Constantine ensured the success of his struggle for imperial power by a series of political murders. Most of these were against members of his own family.

From 312 onward, Constantine used Christianity in his

own political interests. Although he presided over church councils, he was not baptized until 337 when he was nearing death. In certain ways, Constantine helped the church. His political decision to make the church his ally, however, set the stage for an alliance of the church and political power. The church has never fully recovered from this move.

However, this shift surely did not begin with Constantine. From the time of Tertullian and Origen, we find Christians concerned for the preservation of the social order. They desired the well-being of all people. Because of this, they tended to approve of the existing political order.

For an increasing number of Christians, this led to the next step—a willingness to contribute to this order. Some accepted civil office and participated in the military forces. The number of Christians in the Roman army increased toward the end of the third century and the beginning of the fourth. The great persecution under Diocletian began during this period with a purge of Christians in the army.

The number of Christians in the army could not have been very high. No ruler would readily deprive himself of ten percent—or even five percent—of his military power. However, if Constantine tolerated and even favored Christians for political reasons, a considerable number of them must have been in military and civil service.

No doubt when Constantine decided to make Christians allies in his political aspirations, he already saw signs that such an alliance could work. Still, the shift from the earlier nonviolent position would not become complete until 100 years later. In 380 Emperors Theodosius in the East and Gratian in the West established Christianity as the official religion in a joint edict. This change in the Christian attitude toward war was complete by 416 when the empire required all its soldiers to be Christians. This excluded non-Christians from its ranks.

The evolution of the ancient Latin term *paganus* furnishes us with an example of the meaning of this reversal. Up to the year 300, the term meant *civilian* as opposed to *soldier*. Eventually, however, it came to mean *non-Christian* as opposed to *believer*. In similar fashion, Christians had made a complete change from not fighting as soldiers to all soldiers being Christians.

Because of the wide implications of this reversal, some have referred to this process as the "fall of the church." That a major shift had occurred is undeniable. However, to credit Constantine alone with this reversal is to overestimate his importance in the process. It was a complex drama in which both church and empire shared the stage as actors.

However, this change did not come unchallenged by Christians of the period. Basil, who succeeded Eusebius as bishop of Caesarea, complained about the violence of warfare.

> Many gain glory from the valor they show in battle. They go so far as to boast of the murder of their brothers. Indeed, military courage and the triumphal arches erected by a general or the community exist only through the magnitude of murder.[86]

He recognized that church leaders had been pressured to make a concession. Afterward, they no longer called acts of war and capital punishment murder. Even so, Basil required that the soldier "with unclean hands abstain from communion for three years."[87]

The Synod of Arles, called by Constantine in 314, contains an official statement of the church concerning military service. Article 3 states, "Concerning those who throw away their arms in time of peace, it is fitting that they should not be admitted to communion."

During persecution a concession had permitted Christians forced into the army to remain there as soldiers of peace. This meant they could carry out the work and activities required of a noncombatant soldier in time of peace. Of course, they would not become officers, for then they might have to execute the death penalty. In making this concession, the church refused to admit that Christians might shed blood.

We have already noted that the church orders based on the *Apostolic Tradition* had conceded that a Christian might be a soldier. This declaration by the Synod of Arles represents yet another concession. Soldiers who serve in peacetime should stay in the army, rather than cause a scandal by resigning. So the church refused communion to the Christians who cast down their weapons in time of peace. This canon no doubt represents a response to imperial pressures for Christians to serve in the army. However, if soldiers refused to use their weapons in time of war, the church would not censure them.

The Christian church prohibited the shedding of blood for the first four centuries. Recalling its early teaching in this regard, the church for centuries imposed penance on those who had killed in warfare. The canons of Arles show church discipline bending before the pressures of the time and tolerating human weakness. Though Christians should not be soldiers at all, in certain well-defined circumstances, it was possible to tolerate this as the lesser evil. History reminds us, though, that those who consented to be soldiers in time of peace eventually found themselves shedding blood in warfare. At the Synod of Arles, the church made a bargain with the emperor in exchange for his protection. Earlier it had allowed soldiers in the army to remain there in peacetime. Now it was urging them to stay in order to avoid scandal. The church probably felt that the decision was the lowest price at which they could buy the benefits the emperor offered. To the church's credit, it held back from giving permission to kill one's neighbor, even in combat. Although the church did not call for conscientious objection to military service, it still refused to condone bloodshed in wartime. Two factors strongly influenced the church early in the fourth century. These were the rise of the nonviolent monasteries and the growing acceptance of Greek and Roman social values. During this time, the church gradually gave up its earlier opposition to service in the military. The Christian ideals of holiness gradually faded as Christians became more and more at home in the empire.

The former standards were increasingly reserved for the clergy, especially the monastic orders. Therefore, priests were strictly forbidden to shed blood. In fact, ex-soldiers were not to become priests. Now Constantine exempted members of the clergy from all civic and military duties. The state thus permitted a select group of persons to live out the holiness and nonviolence of the Christian ethic. In return, the church gradually decided not to expect such high Christian standards of ordinary Christians.

From the end of the fourth century onward, not only could priests not become soldiers; those who had served in the army could not become priests. Although these rules applied only to the clergy, they recalled the earlier teaching that military service was inappropriate for all Christians. Eventually, the church abandoned the notion that a lasting stain rested upon the person who had once been a soldier. But the exemption granted to the Christian clergy by Constantine from 313 onward became the normal pattern for the future. This practice of excusing Christian clerics from military service has endured to the present in Christendom.

Eusebius contributed largely to the changing attitude of Christians toward war. He reported with approval that Armenian Christians had taken up arms and defeated the imperial adversary of Constantine.[88] Eusebius, of course, interpreted the victories of Constantine as the very work of God.

> Constantine ... and Licinius ... were stirred up by the King of kings, God of the universe and Savior, two men beloved of God, against the two most impious tyrants; and when war was finally engaged, God proved their ally in the most wonderful manner.... Calling in prayer upon God who is in heaven, and his Word, even Jesus Christ the Savior of all, as his ally, he [Constantine] advanced in full force, seeking to secure of the Romans their ancestral liberty.[89]

When imperial troops—now including Christians—committed all sorts of brutal acts in battle, Eusebius did not censure them. They were in his mind divine agents for justice repaying the suffering which believers had earlier endured.[90]

Athanasius (c. 296-373), bishop of Alexandria, outlined a

belief system that included these understandings. The following quotation from his writings shows that Eusebius was not alone in expressing this new Christian interpretation of warfare.

> It is not right to kill, yet in war it is lawful and praiseworthy to destroy the enemy. Accordingly not only are they who have distinguished themselves in the field held worthy of great honors, but monuments are put up proclaiming their achievements. So . . . the same act is at one time and under some circumstances unlawful, while under others and at the right time, it is lawful and permissible.[91]

CHAPTER 11

The Church Makes Peace with the Empire

Ambrose and Augustine

Ambrose and Augustine were active in the leadership of the church in Italy and North Africa during the fourth century. Their writings provided the theological basis for the Constantinian shift. Ambrose was himself an example of this shift.

The son of a military officer, Ambrose became governor in northern Italy. When the bishop of Milan died, the people chose Ambrose as pastor even though he had not been baptized. As bishop he sought to exercise moral influence over the emperor. When the emperor decided to retaliate and massacre the people of Thessalonica, Ambrose disciplined him publicly. He had no doubts about the rightness of employing the power of the empire in the interests of the church. He marveled without question at the changes which had taken place. The princes of the empire, who had once been the persecutors of the church, had become the preachers of the gospel. Ambrose applied texts from the Old Testament to the military task of defending the empire against the barbarians, as well as political adversaries. These are his comments on Psalm 37:15.

> During the latest war, faithless and sacrilegious men challenged one who placed his trust in the Lord [the emperor Theodosius]. They attempted to deprive him of his dominion and they threatened the churches of the Lord with savage persecution. Suddenly, a wind sprang up. It ripped the rebels' shields out of their hands and cast all the javelins and missiles back on the sinner's army. Their opponents had not yet attacked, but already they could not sustain the assault of the wind and were cut down by their own weapons. What is more, the wounds of their spirits were deeper than those of their bodies. They lost heart when they realized that God was fighting against them.[92]

Earlier, concern centered around the question of whether Christians might serve in the army. Now warfare itself was invested with divine sponsorship. When the war was God's, there was no longer any question as to whether Christians might be in the army.

It was Augustine who developed most clearly the implications of the Constantinian shift. He sought to justify theologically the participation of Christians in warfare. He also attempted to limit warfare by insisting that the cause must always be just.

Boniface was a military governor in North Africa. Sorrowing over the death of his wife, he planned to abandon his military career for a monastic life. Augustine tried hard to persuade him to continue to serve God as a soldier.

Augustine based his understanding of the Christian military vocation on the command to love God and the neighbor. He cited both Old and New Testaments to show how military service and the Christian calling could go together. He insisted that the Christian soldier must always seek to establish peace.

> Do not suppose that a person who serves in the army cannot be pleasing to God.... When you are arming yourself for battle, therefore, let this thought be foremost in your mind: even your bodily strength is God's gift. Think about God's gift in this way and do not use it against God. Once you have given your word, you must keep it to the opponent against whom you wage war and all the more to your friend for whom you fight. You must always have peace as your objective and regard war as forced upon you, so that God may free you from this necessity and preserve you in peace. Peace is not sought in order to stir up war; war is waged to serve the peace. You must, therefore, be a peacemaker even in waging war so that by your conquest you may lead those you subdue to the enjoyment of peace.

> "Blessed are the peacemakers," says the Lord, "for they shall be called children of God." How sweet is human peace for the temporal prosperity of mortals; yet how much sweeter is that eternal peace for the eternal salvation of the angels. May it be necessity, therefore, not your own desire, which destroys your attacking enemy. As you respond with ferocity to the rebelling and resisting, so do you owe compassion to the defeated and captured, especially when you no longer fear a disturbance of the peace.[93]

According to Augustine, Christians may justly wage war only when a lawfully established authority orders it. This rules out warfare motivated by evil reasons, such as lust for domination, rebellion, savagery, and cruelty. However, once the Christian has been officially ordered to kill, Augustine believed, he must do so with an untroubled conscience.

What indeed is wrong with war? That people die who will eventually die anyway so that those who survive may be subdued in peace? A coward complains of this, but this does not bother religious people. No, the true evils in warfare are the desire to inflict damage, the cruelty of revenge, disquiet and implacability of spirit, the savagery of rebellion, the lust for domination, and other such things. Indeed, often enough good men are commanded by God or a lawful ruler to wage war precisely in order to punish these things.

When humans undertake war, the person responsible and the reasons for acting are quite important. The natural order which is directed to peace among mortals requires that the ruler take counsel and initiate war; once war has been commanded, the soldiers should serve in it to promote the general peace and safety. No one must ever question the rightness of a war which is waged on God's command. . . . God commands war to drive out, to crush or to subjugate the pride of mortals. . . . No one has any power over them unless it is given from above.

All power comes from God's command or permission. Thus, a just man may rightly fight for the order of civil peace even if he serves under the command of a ruler who is himself irreligious. What he is commanded to do is either clearly not contrary or not clearly contrary to God's precept. The evil of giving the command might make the king guilty, but the order of obedience would keep the soldier innocent. How much more innocently, therefore, might a person engage in [warfare] when he is commanded to fight by God, who can never command anything improperly, as anyone who serves him cannot fail to realize.[94]

Augustine also believed one should use force against Christians who cause splits in the church. For example, when the Donatists of North Africa withdrew from the church, Augustine supported military action against them. He firmly believed the emperor was acting under God's influence, for he was responsible for maintaining peace within the empire. As a Christian ruler, it was his duty to suppress a schism within the church as he would a rebellion in the empire. Augustine found New Testament examples to support his view. He believed Paul had been forcibly converted and that Jesus had recommended the use of force in the parable of the wedding guests. After all, he said, "Go out to the highways and hedges and *compel* people to come in that my house may be filled"(Luke 14:23).

In response to this new context, Emperor Constantine's embrace of Christianity created a new situation for the church. Augustine chose to abandon certain New Testament themes and to emphasize others. In his interpretation of Scripture, he all but abandoned the vision of the presence of the reign of God. According to the Gospels, this reign was so important for Jesus. After Augustine, the kingdom of God came to be understood as primarily future and purely a spiritual concept. The vision of peace foretold by the prophets concerning the Messiah and realized by Jesus in the creation of a new community was no longer an alternative. Augustine, in contrast, spoke of *temporal* peace and *eternal* peace. To him, the first of these was a static imperial peace established by arms. In this sense, he could speak of the emperor and Christian soldiers as peacemakers. *Eternal* peace, however, was a purely spiritual, inner reality which individual believers could enjoy in the present. One could not actually experience this peace until the life to come.

Therefore, according to Augustine's view, Christians engage in warfare to secure an earthly peace. And they suffer the consequences of war as a preparation for their heavenly peace. In fact, from 416 on, only Christians could serve in the army of the empire. The gospel which the church continued to profess was no longer the same gospel of the kingdom which Jesus had proclaimed. The *Pax Romana* of military might had displaced Jesus' gospel of peace.

Epilogue

The first 300 years of the Christian church's history were full of change. Christians related to society and the state in different ways, and this led to changes in the internal life of the church. The church, which began as a messianic movement within first-century Judaism, was at best tolerated. At worst, it was persecuted as a religious minority within the Roman Empire during most of this period. Eventually, under Constantine, the Christian church enjoyed official toleration. Later it won favored status. Finally, it became the official religion of the empire.

The social, economic, and political practices of Christians often determine how the church understands the life, teachings, and death of Jesus. Nowhere is this relationship of cause and effect more clearly seen than in the church's changing attitudes toward warfare and violence. The early church took seriously Jesus' teachings on love toward the enemy and his nonviolent response to evildoers. However, when Christians began to enjoy power, wealth, and prestige, these convictions changed. *Therefore, the theology of the church was brought into line with the practice of Christians.*

For nearly 300 years the church had refused to approve the participation of Christians in warfare. In fact, the church had strongly disapproved of the practice. However, as Christians became increasingly involved in warfare, the church reinterpreted the biblical teachings to justify the participation of Christians in warfare. From then on, Jesus' nonviolent vision of love toward enemies continued only among prophetic minorities both in and out of the church. And that is a story that will be picked up by another writer in the Peace and Justice Series.

Notes

1. Alexander Roberts and James Donaldson, editors, *The Ante-Nicene Fathers*, New York: Charles Scribner's Sons, 1899, vol. 5, pp. 304, 326. Letters 25, 50.

2. Ibid., vol. 4, p. 661. Against Celsus, 8.57.

3. Ibid., vol. 1, pp. 175-176, 254. First Apology, 1.39; Dialogue with Trypho, 110.2-3.

4. Ibid., vol. 1, p. 512. Against Heresies, IV, 34.4.

5. Ibid., vol. 3, p. 154. An Answer to the Jews, 3.9-10.

6. Ibid., vol. 4, pp. 557-558. Against Celsus, 5.33.

7. Ibid., vol. 3, p. 154. An Answer to the Jews, 3.9-10.

8. Ibid., vol. 4, p. 558. Against Celsus, 5.33.

9. Ibid., vol. 1, p. 55. Ephesians, 13.2.

10. Ibid., vol. 1, p. 54. Ephesians, 10.

11. Cyril C. Richardson, editor, *Early Christian Fathers*, The Library of Christian Classics, Philadelphia: Westminster Press, 1953, vol. 1, pp. 70-72. First Clement, 59.4; 60.4

12. Roberts and Donaldson, vol. 1, p. 33. Philippians, 2.

13. Ibid., vol. 2, p. 129. Plea for Christians, 1.

14. Ibid., vol. 2, p. 147. Plea for Christians, 35.4.

15. Ibid., vol. 2, p. 147. Plea for Christians, 35.

16. Ibid., vol. 2, pp. 234-235. The Instructor, I, 12.

17. Ibid., vol. 1, p. 176. First Apology, 39.

18. Ibid., vol. 1, p. 254. Dialogue with Trypho, 110.

19. Ibid., vol. 2, p. 115. Theophilus to Autolycus, III, 14.

20. Ibid., vol. 1, p. 512. Against Heresies, IV, 34.4.

21. Ibid., vol. 3, p. 154. An Answer to the Jews, 3.

22. Ibid., vol. 5, p. 433. On the Dress of Virgins, 11.

23. Ibid., vol. 4, p. 558. Against Celsus, V, 33.

24. Pamphilius Eusebius, *Preparatio Evangelica* (Preparation for the Gospel), I, 4, quoted in Jean-Michel Hornus, *It Is Not Lawful for Me to Fight*, Scottdale, Pa.: Herald Press, 1980, p. 88.

25. Eusebius, VI, 1, quoted in Hornus, p. 88.

26. Athanasius, *De Incarnatione Verbi* (The Incarnation of the Word), 51.4-6; 52.3-5; quoted in Hornus, pp. 88-89.

27. Roberts and Donaldson, vol. 3, p. 93. On the Soldier's Crown, 1.

28. Ibid., vol. 3, pp. 99-100. On the Soldier's Crown, 11.

29. Ibid.

30. *Acta Fructuosus*, 2.2-3, quoted in Hornus, p. 27.

31. Pamphilius Eusebius, *Ecclesiastical History*, trans. C. F. Crusé, London: Henry G. Bohn, 1858, pp. 172-173. V, 5.

32. Roberts and Donaldson, vol. 4, p. 667. Against Celsus, 8.73.

33. Ibid., vol. 4, p. 668. Against Celsus, 8.73.

34. Ibid., vol. 4, p. 665. Against Celsus, 8.68.

35. Ibid., vol. 3, p. 45. Apology, 37.3.

36. Ibid., vol. 3, p. 49. Apology, 42.2.

37. Clement of Alexandria, *Exhortation to the Heathen*, X, 100, quoted in Hornus, p. 124.

38. Roberts and Donaldson, vol. 3, p. 73. On Idolatry, 19.

39. Ibid., vol. 3, pp. 213-215. On the Soul, 33.

40. Ibid., vol. 3, pp. 41-42. Apology, 28.3; 30.1.

41. Ibid., vol. 3, pp. 25-26. Apology 9.5.

42. Ibid., vol. 3, pp. 46-47. Apology 39.7-8.

43. Ibid., vol. 3, p. 101. On the Soldier's Crown, 12.

44. Ibid., vol. 3, pp. 24-25. Apology, 9.8.

45. Ibid., vol. 3, pp. 50-51. Apology, 46.15.

46. Ibid., vol. 3, pp. 54-55. Apology, 50.1-2.

47. Ibid., vol. 4, pp. 467-468. Against Celsus, 3.7-8.

48. Ibid., vol. 4, pp. 667-668. Against Celsus, 8.73.

49. *Apostolic Tradition*, quoted in John Helgeland, Robert J. Daly, and J. Patout Burns, *Christians and the Military: The Early Experience*, Philadelphia: Fortress Press, 1985, p. 37.

50. Eusebius, *Ecclesiastical History*, pp. 271-272. VII, 15.

51. Ibid., pp. 336-339. VIII, 4.

52. The Acts of Maximilian, quoted in Helgeland, et al., pp. 58-59.

53. The Acts of Marcellus, quoted in Hornus, p. 138.

54. The Martyrdom of Julius the Veteran, quoted in Hornus, p.139.

55. Suplicius Severus, Vita Mart., 4.3, quoted in Hornus, p. 144.

56. Vita Mart., 4, 5, 9, quoted in Hornus, p. 145.

57. Roberts and Donaldson, vol. 1, p. 144. Epistle of Barnabas, 11.8.

58. Cyril C. Richardson, vol. 1, p. 171. Teaching of the Twelve Apostles, 1.3.

59. Roberts and Donaldson, vol. 1, p. 8. First Clement, 13.1.

60. Ibid., vol. 1, p. 55. Ephesians, 13.2.

61. Ibid., vol. 1, p. 67. Trallians, 4.2.

62. Allan Menzies, editor, *The Ante-Nicene Fathers*, Grand Rapids: Eerdmans, n.d., vol. 10, pp. 276-277. Apology, 15.5, 10.

63. Roberts and Donaldson, vol. 1, p. 167. First Apology, 14.3.

64. Ibid., vol. 1, p. 168. First Apology, 16.1-4.

65. Ibid., vol. 2, p. 134. Plea for Christians, 11.

66. Ibid., vol. 3, p. 45. Apology, 37.5.

67. Apology, 6.7, quoted in Hornus, p. 215.

68. Roberts and Donaldson, vol. 1, pp. 26-27. Epistle to Diognetus, V-VI.

69. Ibid., vol. 3, p. 108. To Scapula, 5.

70. Ibid., vol. 3, p. 707. De Patientia, 1.

71. Ibid., vol. 3, p. 713. De Patientia, 10.

72. Ibid., 6, quoted in Hornus, p. 216.

73. Roberts and Donaldson, vol. 4, p. 467. Against Celsus, 3.7,8.

74. Ibid., vol. 4, pp. 500-501. Ibid., 4.9.

75. Ibid., vol. 5, pp. 484-486. On the Advantage of Patience, 4, 5-7, 9.

76. Ibid., vol. 5, pp. 488-490. On the Advantage of Patience, 14, 20.

77. Ibid., vol. 5, pp. 462-463, 465. To Demetrianus, 17, 25.

78. Ibid., vol. 7, p. 185. The Divine Institutes, VI, 18.25.

79. Ibid., vol. 7, p. 185. The Divine Institutes, VI, 18, 29-32.

80. De Patientia, 2, quoted in Hornus, p. 220.

81. Eusebius, *Ecclesiastical History*, pp. 373-376. IX, 9.

82. Ibid., pp. 384-386. X, 1.

83. Ibid., pp. 406-408. X, 5.

84. Ibid., pp. 412-413. X, 6-7.

85. Ibid., pp. 417-419. X, 9.

86. Homilies on the Psalms, 61.4, quoted in Hornus, p. 170.

87. Epistles, 188.13, quoted in Hornus, p. 171.

88. Eusebius, *Ecclesiastical History*, pp. 371-373. IX, 8.

89. Ibid., pp. 373-378. IX, 9.

90. Ibid., pp. 382-384. IX, 11.

91. Letter to Amun, quoted in Hornus, p. 183.

92. Exposition of Psalms, 35.25, quoted in Helgeland, et al., pp. 74-75.

93. Letter 189.4,6, quoted in Helgeland, et al., pp. 76-77.

94. Against Faustus, 22.74,75, quoted in Helgeland, et al., pp. 81-82.

For Further Reading

Roland H. Bainton, *Christian Attitudes Toward War and Peace*, New York: Abingdon Press, 1960.

Jean-Michel Hornus, *It Is Not Lawful for Me to Fight: Early Christian Attitudes Toward War, Violence, and the State*, Scottdale, Pennsylvania: Herald Press, 1980.

John Helgeland, Robert J. Daly and J. Patout Burns, *Christians and the Military: The Early Experience*, Philadelphia: Fortress Press, 1985.

The Author

John Driver grew up in Hesston, Kansas, where he graduated from Hesston Academy. He received his B.A. degree from Goshen (Ind.) College in 1950, his B.D. degree from Goshen Biblical Seminary in 1960, and his S.T.M. from Perkins School of Theology in Dallas, Texas, in 1967. He and his wife, Bonita Landis, are the parents of three children.

The Drivers have been serving under the auspices of the Mennonite Board of Missions (Elkhart, Ind.) since 1951. Prior to this John had served with the Mennonite Central Committee in Puerto Rico from 1945 to 1948 and Bonita from 1947 to 1948. They have served as missionaries in Puerto Rico from 1951 to 1966; in Uruguay from 1967 to 1974; in Spain from 1975 to 1980 and again during 1983 and 1984; and in Argentina during 1981.

During their assignment in Uruguay, John served as professor of Church History and New Testament at the Seminario Evangelico Menonita de Teología in Montevideo. He also served the seminary until its closing in late 1974 as dean of studies. Drivers returned to Montevideo in March 1985 at the invitation of the Centro de Estudios of the Mennonite Church in Uruguay where John divides his time between teaching and writing.

John Driver is the author of a number of books which have appeared in both Spanish and English. Among these are *Community and Commitment* (Herald Press, 1976) which first appeared as *Comunidad y Compromiso* (Certeza, Buenos Aires, 1974); *Kingdom Citizens* (Herald Press, 1980), published earlier under the title *Militantes para un Mundo Nuevo* (Ediciones Evangélicas Europeas, Barcelona, 1978); *Becoming God's Community* (The Foundation Series for Adults, 1981); *El Evangelio: Mensaje de Paz* (Mostaza, Zaragoza, Spain, 1984); and *Understanding the Atonement for the Mission of the Church* (Herald Press, 1986).

PEACE AND JUSTICE SERIES

Edited by Elizabeth Showalter and J. Allen Brubaker

This series of books sets forth briefly and simply some important teachings of the Bible about war and peace and how to deal with conflict and injustice. The authors write from within the Anabaptist tradition. This includes viewing the Scriptures as a whole as the believing community discerns God's Word through the guidance of the Spirit. Some of the books reflect biblical, theological, or historical content. Other books in the series show how these principles and insights are lived out in daily life.

1. *The Way God Fights* by Lois Barrett.
2. *How Christians Made Peace with War* by John Driver.
3. *They Loved Their Enemies* by Marian Hostetler.

The books in this series are published in North America by:

Herald Press
616 Walnut Avenue
Scottdale, PA 15683
USA

Herald Press
117 King Street, West
Kitchener, ON N2G 4M5
CANADA

Persons overseas wanting copies for distribution or permission to translate should write to the Scottdale address listed above.